I THOUGHT OF IT WHILE SHAVING

David & Annette J   *editors*

Harold Shaw Publishers
Wheaton, Illinois

Copyright © 1992 by Harold Shaw Publishers

Editors: David & Annette LaPlaca

Cover, design, & illustrations © 1992 by Turnbaugh & Associates

ISBN 0-87788-387-4

Library of Congress Cataloging-in-Publication Data

I thought of it while shaving : ideas for devoted dads / Annette LaPlaca, editor.
    p.   cm.
  Includes bibliographical references.
  ISBN 0-87788-387-4
  1. Fathers—Quotations, maxims, etc. 2. Fatherhood—Quotations, maxims, etc. I. LaPlaca, Annette Heinrich, 1964-
PN6084.F3I2   1992
306.874'2—dc20   91-41549
                                      CIP

---

99 98 97 96 95 94 93 92

10 9 8 7 6 5 4 3 2

CONTENTS

CELEBRATING FATHERHOOD

What is a father? To his child, he is strength, security,
example, and number-one friend. It's a
great calling, so celebrate the gift of your fatherhood!

A father is a gift from God
From which we learn to be
Patient, strong, and loving,
Filled with integrity.
Byron P. Tousignant

■

There is no more vital calling or vocation for men than
fathering.   *John R. Throop, in* Parents and Children

■

Nothing I've ever done has given me more joys and rewards
than being a father to my five.   *Bill Cosby,* Fatherhood

■

A father is a person who is forced to endure childbirth ✓
without an anaesthetic.   *Robert C. Savage,* Pocket Quips

■

Directly after God in Heaven comes Papa.   *Wolfgang
Amadeus Mozart, as a child*

■

The glory of children is their father.   *Proverbs 17:6, NKJV*

1

■

√ A dad is a fellow who has replaced the currency in his
wallet with snapshots of his family. *Presbyterian Life*

■

All that I ask of the Lord to do
Is to see that the mother comes safely through.
And guard the baby and have it well,
With a perfect form and a healthy yell
And a pair of eyes and a shock of hair,
Then, boy or girl—its dad won't care. *Edgar Guest*

■

I can always count on getting one thing for Father's Day—
all the bills from Mother's Day! *Milton Berle*

■

Being a parent is better than a course on theology. Being a
father is teaching me that when I am criticized, injured or

afraid, there is a Father who is ready to comfort me. There is a Father who will hold me until I'm better, help me until I can live with the hurt and who won't go to sleep when I'm afraid of waking up and seeing the dark. Ever. *Max Lucado, "Band-Aids and Fwashlights," in* Marriage Partnership

■

A man who deliberately becomes a parent does so in the full knowledge that there are certain physical hazards involved. . . . He is condemning himself to a life in which every so often he is going to fall over a bicycle in a dark hallway, and he is going to rise from his easy chair every once in a while with a gummy piece of hard candy sticking to his pants, and he is also going to step on a skate, left where it had no business, and fall on the back of his neck on a hardwood floor. . . . They have a thousand ways of booby-trapping you. *Harold H. Martin,* Father's Day Comes Once a Year—and Then It Always Rains

■

The words a father speaks to his children in the privacy of the home are not overheard at the time, but as in whispering galleries, they will be heard at the end and by posterity. *Jean Paul Richter*

■

If a poll were taken of children asking why they thought their parents had children, 12% of them would say they got bored watching television, 26% would say it was a 4-H project that got out of hand, and 62% would swear adults had kids to get out of doing their own dishes. *Erma Bombeck,* Family: The Ties That Bind . . . and Gag!

■

A small boy's definition: "Father's Day is just like Mother's Day, only you don't spend as much on the present." *Toronto Star*

■

He knows, without doubt, that in wife and child he has the only treasures that really matter anyway. *Lewis Grizzard,* Chili Dawgs Always Bark at Night

■

Only a dad, but he gives his all
To smooth the way for his children small;
Doing, with courage stern and grim,
The deeds that his father did for him.
These are the lines that for him I pen,
Only a dad, but the best of men. *Anonymous*

■

No man can possibly know what life means, what the world means, what anything means, until he has a child and loves it. And then the whole universe changes and nothing will ever again seem exactly as it seemed before. *Lafcadio Hearn*

■

To be a successful father there's one absolute rule: when you have a kid, don't look at it for about two years. *Ernest Hemingway*

4

■

For reasons I can't explain, I really like being a parent. It's just that there's a lot more to it than I expected. *Dave Barry,* Dave Barry Turns 40

■

The very words "my father" always make me smile.
Angela Carter

■

My father was not a failure. After all, he was the father of a President of the United States. *Harry S. Truman*

■

Living with a child is, literally, an incomparable experience. It's a gift that has made my life what it is today. I couldn't live without it. *Frank Ferrara,* On Being Father

■

Mother nature, in her infinite wisdom, has instilled within each of us a powerful biological instinct to reproduce; this is her way of assuring that the human race, come what may, will never have any disposable income. *Dave Barry,* Dave Barry Turns 40

■

To the world he's nothing special,
Never loud his praises ring;
But in this devoted circle,
He is master, lord, and king.
Maurice J. Ronayne, "Portrait of Dad"

■

As soon as you become a father, your job is cut out for you. It is probably the most eternally significant job you will ever have. *Paul Heidebrecht, in* Parents and Children

■

Parenthood remains the greatest single preserve of the amateur. *Alvin Toffler,* Future Shock

■

In an obstetrician's office: "To heir is human." *Saturday Evening Post*

■

Two-plus years into this fatherhood business, I know at least that what kids require of their fathers is a lot of attention, a lot of love, and, I suspect, if mine ever reach the age of understanding, a lot of that, too. *Carey Winfrey*

■

When I was a boy of fourteen, my father was so ignorant I could hardly stand to have the old man around. But when I got to be twenty-one, I was astounded at how much he had learned in seven years. *Mark Twain*

■ ■ ■ ■ ■ ■ ■ ■ ■ ■ ■ ■ ■ ■ ■

CELEBRATING CHILDREN

Kids—what would we do without them? Children sweeten our days with unhesitating trust and affection and refresh our spirits with their enthusiastic approach to life and their vast curiosity for all things new and different. They're treasured gifts from a loving God.

Sons are a heritage from the LORD,
  children a reward from him.
Like arrows in the hands of a warrior
  are sons born in one's youth.
Blessed is the man
  whose quiver is full of them.
Psalm 127:3-5

■

The fortunes of father
Are found in the ones
He can proudly point out
As his daughters and sons!
Frank H. Keith

■

Children are children are children—and running, exploring, playing, climbing, and noisemaking just come with the territory. *Pamela Barden, in* Parents and Children

■

Children are gleeful barbarians. *Joseph Morgenstern*

7

■

Have you taken time lately to thank God for these wonderful gifts you call your children? Or has life been so busy that you see them only as challenges, as mischiefs, as time eaters, as heavy responsibilities, or as headaches and problems? *Tim Hansel,* What Kids Need Most in a Dad

■

A baby is an inestimable blessing and bother. *Mark Twain*

■

He took a little child and had him stand among them. Taking him in his arms, he said to them, "Whoever welcomes one of these little children in my name welcomes me; and whoever welcomes me does not welcome me but the one who sent me." *Mark 9:36-37*

■

Those of you who do not live around children may not know what a Big Wheel is. It is a tricycle-like vehicle made of plastic. When it is pedaled across pavement by a four-year-old, it makes a sound unbearable to the adult ear. *Lewis Grizzard,* Kathy Sue Loudermilk, I Love You

■

Childhood is where "competition" is a baseball game and "responsibility" is a paper route. *Erma Bombeck*

■

Children and bedtime—often two incompatible entities. *Vicki Huffman,* Plus Living

Between the dark and the daylight,
When the night is beginning to lower,
Comes a pause in the day's occupations
That is known as the children's hour.
Henry Wadsworth Longfellow

Our greatest gift to the world in which we live is the gift of
children, the heirs we hope will carry on and improve
whatever we have done to build that world. *Leonard and
Thelma Spinrad*

■

Any parent knows that a newborn is just a loud voice at one end and no sense of responsibility at the other. *Roy Fairchild*

■

Most things have an escape clause . . . but children are forever. *Lewis Grizzard,* Chili Dawgs Always Bark at Night

■

God superintended your child's construction even down to the tips of his fingers. And just as surely as that child has his very own fingerprints, he has a lot of his very own other things as well—personality, perspective, and problems. He is as special as his fingerprints. *Cliff Schimmels,* Oh No! Maybe My Child Is Normal!

■

Little boys tend to be—and I say this as a loving father who would not trade his son for anything in the world— jerks. . . . when we look at actual children, no matter how they are raised, we notice immediately that little girls are in fact smaller versions of real human beings, whereas little boys are Pod People from the Planet Destructo. *Dave Barry,* Dave Barry Turns 40

■

Life is a flame that is always burning itself out, but it catches fire again every time a child is born. *George Bernard Shaw*

10

Let us look upon our children, let us love them and train them, as children of the covenant and children of the promise—these are the children of God. *Andrew Murray,* How to Raise Your Children for Christ

■

Ask your child what he wants for dinner only if he's buying. *Fran Lebowitz,* Social Studies

■

Definition of a child: a thing that stands halfway between an adult and a television set. *Unknown*

■

Children are not so different from kites. . . . Children were created to fly. But they need wind—the undergirding and strength that comes from unconditional love, encouragement, and prayer. *Gigi Graham Tchividjian, "Catch the Wind," in* Christian Parenting Today

■

What I have no patience with is the growing tendency among psychologists to insist that children are really *people*, little adults—just like the rest of us, only smaller. . . . We all know better than that. Children are different—mentally, physically, spiritually, quantitively, qualitively, and furthermore they're all a little bit nuts. *Jean Kerr,* Please Don't Eat the Daisies

■

Jesus said, "Let the little children come to me, and do not hinder them, for the kingdom of heaven belongs to such as these." *Matthew 19:14*

■

Children are today's investment and tomorrow's dividend. *Unknown*

■

Kids are great. They are exciting. Their potential is simply phenomenal. And in any given family there is the potential to change this world for God. *Maxine Hancock,* Creative, Confident Children

■

There is so much that is beautiful and good to wake up to. Our children drive us toward this awakening. *Polly Berrien Berends,* Whole Child/Whole Parent

■

Our children—even when smeared with mud or misdeeds—are God's gracious gift to us. *David Grant, "A Grace Assignment," in* Christian Parenting Today

■

Of all people, children are the most imaginative. They abandon themselves without reserve to every illusion. *J.B. Macauley*

·

God did not create a boring world. If we wonder at the
uniqueness of a snowflake, how much more must we
stand in awe of the infinite variety we find in human
beings? Each child is more than an addition to the family.
Through the gifts he or she brings, all family members are
enriched. In a loving family, they all win.   *Joseph and Lois
Bird,* To Live as Family

·

It is not a slight thing when they, who are so fresh from
God, love us.   *Charles Dickens*

·

I will never understand children. I never pretended to.   *Erma
Bombeck,* If Life Is a Bowl of Cherries, What Am I Doing in the Pits?

·

The childhood shows the man,
As morning shows the day.   *John Milton*

·

All God's children are not beautiful. Most of God's
children are, in fact, barely presentable.   *Fran Lebowitz,*
Social Studies

·

God does not give bad gifts and good gifts; He simply
gives different gifts. And when we can accept this in our

children, we'll have come a long way toward understanding their uniqueness, and toward achieving family harmony. *Jay Kesler,* Ten Mistakes Parents Make with Teenagers

■

Every child comes with the message that God is not yet discouraged of man. *Tagore*

■

Every child who comes into the world presents a new possibility for lifting the destiny of the human race. *Anna B. Mow,* Preparing Your Child to Love God

■

We are responsible to God because our children are gifts from Him. There is no person alive—in or out of the womb—who is not a gift to his parents from God. It is impossible to comprehend the immense value of our lives and souls when we realize this one simple truth: We are all gifts from God. *Renee Jordan,* Parents, Love Your Children

■

Children aren't happy with nothing to ignore,
And that's what parents were created for. *Ogden Nash*

■

Adolescence is the age at which children stop asking questions because they know all the answers. *Jo Petty,* Apples of Gold

■

Children are a great comfort in your old age—and they
help you to reach it faster, too.   *Lionel M. Kaufman*

■

A child more than all other gifts
That earth can offer to declining man
Brings hope with it, and forward-looking thoughts.
William Wordsworth

■

There are two classes of travel—first class and with
children.   *Robert Benchley*

■

Every child born into the world is a new thought of God,
an ever-fresh and radiant possibility.   *Kate Douglas Wiggin*

■

A child is not a vase to be filled, but a lamp to be lighted.
Unknown

■

If you have lost your faith in yourself, just go out and get
acquainted with a small child. Win his love and your faith
will come stealing back to you before you know it.   *Nick
Kenny*

■

Where children are, there is the golden age.   *Novalis*

■

A baby is God's opinion that the world should go on.
Carl Sandburg

■

Children are God's small interpreters.   *John Greenleaf Whittier*

■

Children in a family are like flowers in a bouquet. There is always one determined to face in an opposite direction from the way the arranger desires.   *Marcelene Cox, in* Oh No! Maybe My Child Is Normal!

■

Children sweeten labors, but they make misfortunes more bitter; they increase the cares of life, but they mitigate the remembrance of death.   *Francis Bacon,* Of Parents and Children

■

And he said: "I tell you the truth, unless you change and become like little children, you will never enter the kingdom of heaven. Therefore, whoever humbles himself like this child is the greatest in the kingdom of heaven."
Matthew 18:2-4

■

A child is a most desirable pest.   *Max Gralmich*

■

The child is father of the man.   *William Wordsworth*

■

On the bright face of a child one can capture
The old hope and faith we would seek to redeem . . .
The beauty we once saw, the sweet childish rapture
In the eyes of a small child aglow with a dream.   *Ruth B.
Field*

■

The child, the seed, the grain of corn,
The acorn on the hill,
Each for some separate end is born
In season fit, and still
Each must in strength arise to work
The Almighty will.
Robert Louis Stevenson

■

The children of today will be the architects of our
country's destiny tomorrow.   *James A. Garfield*

■

Children today are tyrants. They contradict their parents,
gobble their food, and tyrannize their teachers.   *Socrates
(470-399 B.C.)*

■

I like children. Maybe that's a little strong. I don't have
anything against children, and from what limited
knowledge I have of them, there is apparently at least
some appeal to their company. They seem to forgive easi-

17

ly, like dogs, and I am impressed by that. When they first awaken, they look around for somebody to hold them. I know the feeling.

Lewis Grizzard, Kathy Sue Loudermilk, I Love You

■

Adolescence is that period in a kid's life when his or her parents become more difficult.   *Ryan O'Neal*

■

For the first two years of a child's life you try to get him to talk. For the next ten years you devote your life to getting him to shut up. For the remainder of his life you try to get his lips moving again and sound coming from his throat.   *Erma Bombeck,* I Lost Everything in the Post-Natal Depression

■

When I was kidnapped, my parents snapped into action. They rented out my room.   *Woody Allen*

■

It's been my observation that as soon as a boy has become housebroken and a pleasure to have about, he is no longer about. He's in school all the time.   *Jean Kerr,* How I Got to Be Perfect

■

Pretty much all the honest truth-telling there is in the world is done by children.   *Oliver Wendell Holmes*

Children are our most valuable natural resource. *Herbert Hoover*

What was wonderful about childhood is that anything in it was a wonder. It was not merely a world full of miracles, it was a miraculous world. *G.K. Chesterton,* Autobiography

The one thing children wear out faster than shoes is parents. *John J. Plomp*

It will be worth the sacrifice, knowing you've done all you can to prepare your children to go out and make their way, on their own, in the Real World. Although they'll

probably decide it's easier just to move back in with you.
Dave Barry, Dave Barry Turns 40

■

Children are the only earthly possessions we can take with us to heaven.   *Robert C. Savage,* Pocket Quips

■

There is this to be said about children. They keep you feeling old.   *Jean Kerr,* How I Got to Be Perfect

■

Then our sons in their youth
   will be like well-nurtured plants,
and our daughters will be like pillars
   carved to adorn a palace. . . .
Blessed are the people whose God is the LORD.
Psalm 144:12, 15

■ ■ ■ ■ ■ ■ ■ ■ ■ ■ ■ ■ ■ ■ ■ ■

GODLY LEADERSHIP

Fathers are God's designated family administrators. A dad's
leadership skills are nowhere more crucial than at home.
Take time to analyze and polish your father/leader techniques.

As for me and my household, we will serve the LORD.
Joshua 24:15

■

In a unique sort of way, God calls upon the man to be the
family's governor, its accountable representative to make
sure that God's laws are being followed, that people in
that family have every opportunity to experience all that
the Creator intends for them to be.   *Gordon MacDonald*, The
Effective Father

■

My primary role is not to be the boss and just look good
but to be a servant leader who enables and enhances my
family to be their best.   *Tim Hansel*, What Kids Need Most in a
Dad

■

A good coach is the key to building a winning team. It is
your spirit, your drive, your enthusiasm, and your exper-
tise that will ultimately make the difference between success or failure.   *Kay Kuzma*, Prime-Time Parenting

■

When the modeling is as it should be, there is seldom much trouble from those who fall under the shadow of the leader. Strengthening your grip on the family may start with an unguarded appraisal of the leadership your family is expected to follow. *Charles R. Swindoll,* Strengthening Your Grip

■

There's no substitute for the sense of satisfaction that comes from watching as your children, under your steady, guiding hand, develop from tiny, helpless Frequent Barfer modules into full-grown, self-reliant young adults fully capable of crashing your car into a day-care center. *Dave Barry,* Dave Barry Turns 40

■

Plant seeds of spiritual truth so that they grow in your child's fertile mind—and bear good fruit. *Rita Schweitz*

■

Male leadership does not suggest a dominating, high-handed action, based on selfish motives. To be successful in the family the father must have the welfare of each family member at heart and his decisions and plans must be based upon what is best for them. He carefully considers their viewpoint and feelings, especially those of his wife. They try to work things out together. *Helen Andelin,* All About Children

The father is the head of a unit of people launched on an exploration of life and all the things God has placed in the world for us to discover and enjoy. *Gordon MacDonald,* The Effective Father

■

Let love and faithfulness never leave you; bind them around your neck, write them on the tablet of your heart. Then you will win favor and a good name in the sight of God and man. *Proverbs 3:3-4*

■

He that thinketh he leadeth, and hath no one following him—he is only out for a walk. *Unknown*

■

If America is going to survive the incredible stresses and dangers it now faces, it will be because husbands and fathers again place their families at the highest level on their system of priorities, reserving a portion of their time and energy for leadership within their homes. *James Dobson,* Straight Talk to Men and Their Wives

■

Just how difficult it is to be someone's parent is one of the best kept secrets around. *Polly Berrien Berends,* Whole Child/Whole Parent

23

•

Gracious God . . . Teach us, teach all Christian parents, to realize that if there is one thing in which Thou hast an interest, in which Thou givest abundant grace, in which Thou askest and aidest faith, it is for a believing fatherhood, for our receiving our children from Thee and for Thee. O God, enlighten and sanctify our hearts to realize that the fruit of our body is to be the heir of Thy promise. *Andrew Murray,* How to Raise Your Children for Christ

•

Action springs not from thought, but from a readiness for responsibility. *Dietrich Bonhoeffer,* Letters and Papers from Prison

•

It has been said that paternity is a career imposed on you one fine morning without any inquiry as to your fitness for it. That is why there are so many fathers who have children, but so few children who have fathers. *Adlai Stevenson*

•

Responsibility should be shouldered; you cannot carry it under your arm. *Unknown*

•

God has charged men with the responsibility for providing leadership in their homes and families. Leadership in the form of loving authority, leadership in the form of financial management, leadership in the form of spiritual training, and leadership in maintaining the marital relationship.   *James Dobson,* Straight Talk to Men and Their Wives

■

I can delegate a lot of my responsibilities at work, but I cannot delegate my hopes for my family. The primary values, attitudes, skills, and competencies that my children will grow up with will be learned (or not learned) in my home.   *Tim Hansel,* What Kids Need Most in a Dad

■

Much as God the Father created the earth by the power of his words, you as a father create a world for your children by what you say. . . . A father's words are like a thermostat that sets the temperature in the house.   *Paul Lewis, "Power Talk," in* Christian Parenting Today

■

God has given me three children, and ever since I can remember I have directed them to Christ. . . . I would rather lead them to Jesus than give them the wealth of the world.   *Dwight L. Moody*

■

To be successful parents, we must first love the Word of God.   *George Sweeting*

■

Making babies may be an innate skill, but being a competent father is not. It is learned. . . . If we dads are going to make it, we have to give the same diligence to fathering that it takes to be competent as a plumber, pilot, or any other professional. *Paul Lewis, "Stuff No One Ever Told Me,"* *in* Christian Parenting Today

■

Whole-life stewardship means putting the purposes of God at the very center of our lives and families. *Tom Sine*

■

The fatherhood of God is the summing up of the incomprehensible mystery and glory of the divine Being. And of this fatherhood the father of the family on earth is to be the image and the likeness. In the life he imparts to his child . . . in the love in which family life finds its happiness, the home and fatherhood of earth are the image of the heavenly. *Andrew Murray,* How to Raise Your Children for Christ

■

Help us to the stature of good parenthood, O God. . . . Still our voices and smooth from our brows all that mars infectious serenity and joy in living; rather let our faces so shine that these adult years will seem to them a promised land toward which to strive. . . . As we see them striding forward eagerly, self-sure, friendly, and in good conscience, our grateful hearts will swell with joy. *Marion B. Durfee*

■ ■ ■ ■ ■ ■ ■ ■ ■ ■ ■ ■ ■ ■ ■ ■

FATHERLOVE

Your relationship with your child is one-of-a-kind—
no one else will ever be "Dad" to him or her.
So demonstrate the heavenly Father's never-ending
love by showing your child your own unconditional love.

A father is a man who is always learning how to love. He
knows that his love must grow and change because his
children change. *Tim Hansel,* What Kids Need Most in a Dad

■

Love isn't just happiness in ideal situations with everything going according to daydreams of family life or married life or parent-child closeness and confidence. Love
has *work* to do! Hard and self-sacrificial work. *Edith
Schaeffer,* What Is a Family?

■

Parenthood is just the world's most intensive course in
love. *Polly Berrien Berends,* Whole Child/Whole Parent

■

After all is said and done, the most important part of a
child's background at any time is the love and companion-
ship of his parents. Children will leave their most precious
toys or the most fascinating game for a romp with
Mommy and Daddy. The best gift parents can give
children is themselves. *Annie Laurie von Tun*

27

If a man can't get a little sentimental about kids, what *can* he get sentimental about? *Harold H. Martin,* Father's Day Comes Once a Year—and Then It Always Rains

Children need love, especially when they do not deserve it. *Harold S. Hulbert*

I realized that if my children were to know Christ's love, then I, as their father, needed to experience more of

28

Christ's love and make that love visible. *John Drescher,* If I
Were Starting My Family Again

■

May mine be a family faith, exercising its influence on
my home, gaining and training all to walk with me. . . .
May mine be a truly consecrated home. *Andrew Murray,*
How to Raise Your Children for Christ

■

Love is active and sincere; courageous, patient, faithful,
prudent, and manly. *Thomas à Kempis*

■

I know my father loved me—my mother told me he did. It
would have been wonderful if he had told me himself
more often. Maybe he didn't understand how much I
needed to hear those words. *Vicki Huffman,* Plus Living

■

Love is patient, love is kind . . . it is not self-seeking, it is
not easily angered, it keeps no record of wrongs . . . It
always protects, always trusts, always hopes, always per-
severes. Love never fails. *1 Corinthians 13:4-8*

■

Unconditional love is loving a child no matter what. No
matter what the child looks like. No matter what his as-
sets, liabilities, handicaps. No matter what we expect him
to be, and most difficult, no matter how he acts. *Ross
Campbell,* How to Really Love Your Child

The first duty of love is to listen. *Paul Tillich*

The only authority that has an intrinsic right to be obeyed is the authority of a great love for our children that will express and commend to them the greater love of the Heavenly Father. *Thomas Small,* The Forgotten Father

The great man is he who dares not lose his child's heart.
Mencius

It's not uncommon today to find father as nurturer, willing to put urgent matters aside for what he agrees is more important—an active role as family member. . . . He seeks out more active and creative roles in childrearing. *Leo Buscaglia*

Love cannot be wasted. It makes no difference where it is bestowed, it always brings in big returns. *Unknown*

The first, most fundamental right of childhood is the right to be loved. The child comes into the world alone, defenseless, without resource. Only love can stand between his infant helplessness and the savagery of a harsh world. *Paul Hanly Furfey,* The Church and the Child

■

Love conquers all things except poverty and toothache.
Mae West

■

When we love something it is of value to us, and when something is of value to us we spend time with it, time enjoying it and time taking care of it. . . . So it is when we love children; we spend time admiring them and caring for them. We give them our time. *M. Scott Peck,* The Road Less Traveled

■

Only a wise man knows how to love. *Unknown*

■

The ability to love is the heart of the matter. That is how we must measure our success or failure at being parents. *Gloria Vanderbilt*

■

As a father has compassion on his children, so the LORD has compassion on those who fear him. *Psalm 103:13*

■

Children desperately need to know—and to hear in ways they understand and remember—that they're loved and valued by Mom and Dad. *Gary Smalley and Paul Trent,* The Language of Love

■

If a parent neglects to give a child love, no one else can substitute for that gap. The child will suffer. Parental love is of primary importance. . . . A parent can never give too much love to a child.   *Kay Kuzma,* Prime-Time Parenting

■

Love must be tough.   *James Dobson*

■

Traditional prescriptions for fatherhood are too limiting to suit our changing times. The only emotional parenting image a father usually has to go by is that of "mother." But the nurturing feelings expressed by fathers are not simply mother's feelings transferred. They are feelings that reflect male attitudes and viewpoints. Men are not looking to take on mothering roles but to respond as fathers, as men, as themselves.   *Cecilia Worth,* The Birth of a Father

■

In the Christian sense, love is not primarily an emotion but an act of the will.   *Frederick Buechner,* Wishful Thinking

■

Love is the crowning grace of humanity, the holiest right of the soul, the golden link which binds us to duty and truth, the redeeming principle that chiefly reconciles the heart of life, and is prophetic of eternal good.   *Petrarch*

■ ■ ■ ■ ■ ■ ■ ■ ■ ■ ■ ■ ■ ■ ■

TRAIN UP A CHILD

Guiding your children into responsible, godly adulthood
is the most important work of your life.
Pray for wisdom as you seek to train your children.

A wise son maketh a glad father.   *Proverbs 10:1, KJV*

■

A man's children and his garden both reflect the amount
of weeding done during the growing season.   *Unknown*

■

Train a child in the way he should go, and when he is old
he will not turn from it.   *Proverbs 22:6*

■

The best way for a man to train up a child in the way he
should go is to travel that way himself.   *Unknown*

■

God is always our model and source for becoming positive parents.   *Don Highlander,* Positive Parenting

■

Raising kids is part joy and part guerilla warfare.   *Ed Asner*

■

Before I got married I had six theories about bringing up
children; now I have six children and no theories.   *Lord
Rochester*

■

We can fly jet airplanes, broadcast color television, and make atomic power, but we're not so sure about how to bring up children. *Herbert V. Prochnow*

■

One father is more than a hundred schoolmasters. *Unknown*

■

When we train our children, we initiate techniques that bring about a submissive will. We also discover ways to develop our child's taste so that he delights in things that are wholesome and right. None of this is naturally known by a child. These are things parents need to inculcate during those growing-up years in the home. *Charles R. Swindoll,* You and Your Child

■

The quality of a child's relationship with his or her father seems to be the most important influence in deciding how that person will react to the world. *John Nicholson*

■

To us as parents is entrusted the vital task of character development—of imprinting the distinctive stamp of godliness upon the lives of our children. *Maxine Hancock,* Creative, Confident Children

■

Some parents bring up their children on thunder and lightning, but thunder and lightning never yet made anything grow. Rain or sunshine cause growth—quiet penetrating forces that develop life. *Unknown*

■

Raising children is a creative endeavor, an art rather than a science. *Bruno Bettelheim,* A Good Enough Parent

■

Each child is unique, a special creation of God with talents, abilities, personality, preferences, dislikes, potentials, strengths, weakness, and skills that are his or her own. As parents, we must seek to identify these in each of our children and help them become the persons God intended. *Dave Veerman, in* Parents and Children

■

Fathers, do not exasperate your children; instead, bring them up in the training and instruction of the Lord. *Ephesians 6:4*

■

Remember the immortal words of that philosopher and father, Moss Hart, who once announced that in dealing with *his* children he kept one thing in mind: "We're bigger than they are, and it's *our* house." *Jean Kerr,* Please Don't Eat the Daisies

■

Discipline is a long-term process. It's the molding of character and values, self-control, and relationship style which takes place throughout childhood and which helps produce the person that the child eventually becomes in adulthood. *Philip Osborne,* Parenting for the 90s

■

Prime-time parents are parents who consider every minute with their children prime time to communicate the message of parental love, interest, and care. *Kay Kuzma,* Prime-Time Parenting

■

To show a child what has once delighted you, to find the child's delight added to your own, so that there is now a double delight seen in the glow of trust and affection, this is happiness. *J.B. Priestly*

■

The only way to get this world back on track is to go back to the basics: How we raise our kids. *Lee Iacocca*

■

Train is a word of deep importance for every parent to understand. Training is not telling, not teaching, not commanding, but something higher than all these. It is not only *telling* a child what to do, but also *showing him how to do it* and seeing that it is *done.* *Andrew Murray,* How to Raise Your Children for Christ

■

Your child is watching too much television if there exists the possibility that he might melt down. *Fran Lebowitz,* Social Studies

■

Folly is bound up in the heart of a child,
  but the rod of discipline will drive it far from him. . . .
Discipline your son, and he will give you peace;
  he will bring delight to your soul.
Proverbs 22:15; 29:17

■

If you bungle raising your children, I don't think whatever
else you do well matters very much.   *Jacquelyn Kennedy*

■

The most effective thing we can do for our children and
families is pray for them.   *Anthony T. Evans,* Guiding Your
Family in a Misguided World

■

The goal of disciplining our children is to encourage
their growth as respectful, responsible, self-disciplined
individuals.   *Don H. Highlander,* Parents Who Encourage,
Children Who Succeed

■

Of all the gifts that a parent can give a child, the gift of learning to make good choices is the most valuable and long-
lasting.   *Pat Holt and Grace Ketterman,* Choices Are Not Child's Play

■

In spite of six thousand manuals on child raising in the
bookstores, child raising is still a dark continent and no
one really knows anything. You just need a lot of love and

luck—and, of course, courage because you'll be spending years in fear of your kids. *Bill Cosby*, Fatherhood

■

Self-esteem isn't a lesson you teach; it's a quality you nurture. *Dr. Ronald Levant and John Kelly*, Between Father and Child

■

Love and discipline are the foundation of training your child. Love is essential from infancy through growing years. It would be difficult for your child to become a happy, emotionally secure person without generous amounts of love! Without discipline you can not hope to teach your child to be a respectful, competent, and responsible adult. *J. Allen Peterson*, Two Become One

■

Babies come into the world with no instructions, and you pretty much have to assemble them on your own. They are maddeningly complex, and there are no guaranteed formulas that work in every instance. *James Dobson*, Parenting Isn't for Cowards

■

The best parenting skills come most naturally when the parents are on their knees. *Julie Bakke*

■

When you listen to your children, you are paying them a compliment. By listening, you increase their feelings of self-respect and self-worth. *Dean and Grace Merrill*, Together at Home

■

If you are going to do anything permanent for the
average man, you must begin before he is a man.
Theodore Roosevelt

■

Training a child is more or less a matter of pot luck.   *Rod
Maclean*

■

He who spares the rod hates his son,
  but he who loves him is careful to discipline him. . . .
Discipline your son, for in that there is hope.
Proverbs 13:24; 19:18

■

As I take God's view of my children, I see them being
formed into his image and receive it as a finished matter. I
have seen the end from the middle and the matter is set-
tled.   *Jack Taylor,* One Home Under God

■

We need to expose our children to aggressive, vital,
dynamic Christianity and continue to pray for them.
Prayer accomplishes more than anything else.   *Bill Bright,
in* How to Raise Christian Kids in a Non-Christian World

■

As we accept our children, we free them to be who they
are in a world that is trying to tell them every day to be
someone else.   *Tim Hansel,* What Kids Need Most in a Dad

■

Interest your kids in bowling. Get them off the streets and into the alleys. *Don Rickles*

■

The training of children is a profession where we must know how to lose time in order to gain it. *Rousseau*

■

The fundamental defect of fathers is that they want their children to be a credit to them. *Bertrand Russell, in* New York Times

■

We reap what we sow, more than we sow, later than we sow. *Charles Stanley,* How to Keep Your Kids on Your Team

■

The atmosphere in which children grow to fullest maturity is marked with affirmation—recognizing what a child is, appreciation—recognizing what a child does, and affection—recognizing ways to show love for a child. *Gordon MacDonald,* The Effective Father

■

Only be careful, and watch yourselves closely so that you do not forget the things your eyes have seen or let them slip from your heart as long as you live. Teach them to your children and to their children after them.
Deuteronomy 4:9

■

Love the LORD your God with all your heart and with ✓ all your soul and with all your strength. These commandments that I give you today are to be upon your hearts. Impress them on your children. Talk about them when you sit at home and when you walk along the road, when you lie down and when you get up.
Deuteronomy 6:5-7

■

If a child lives with friendliness he learns that the world is a nice place in which to live. *Unknown*

■

If it is desirable that children be kind, appreciative, and pleasant, those qualities should be taught—not hoped for. If we want to see honesty, truthfulness, and unselfishness in our offspring, then these characteristics should be conscious objectives of our early instructional process. *James Dobson,* Dare to Discipline

■

In praising or loving a child we love and praise not that which is, but that which we hope for. *Goethe*

■

The hardest part of raising children is teaching them to ride bicycles. . . . A shaky child on a bicycle for the first time needs both support and freedom. The realization that this is what the child will always need can hit hard. *Sloan Wilson*

■

It is better to keep children to their duty by a sense of honor and by kindness than by fear.
Terence

■

Character is not something highly valued in this society. Our children will get little or no reinforcement for having strong character outside the home, so it is most important that the development of strong character be emphasized and rewarded in the home. *Charles Stanley,* How to Keep Your Kids on Your Team

■

You don't raise heroes; you raise sons. And if you treat them like sons, they'll turn out to be heroes, even if it's just in your own eyes. *Walter Schirra, Sr.*

■

The most influential of educational factors is the conversation in a child's home. *William Temple*

■

Let love be your guide! A relationship that is characterized by genuine love and affection is likely to be a healthy one, even though some parental mistakes and errors are inevitable. *James Dobson,* The Strong-Willed Child

■

Place before children nothing but what is simple, lest you spoil the taste—and nothing that is not innocent, lest you spoil the heart. *Joseph Joubet*

■

Because we love our children we should be patient with them. Just think how patient God is with us. How He waits in love until we decide to come to Him. . . . How He tolerates again and again our sinning and is joyful when we ask to be forgiven! How tirelessly He listens to our excuses . . . watches our stumbling feet so that He can catch us when we fall! Our Heavenly Father never says, "I told you so!" Instead He sets us back on our feet with tender, loving hands. How precious is the patience of the Lord, and how endless His mercies! We need to be patient with

our children in the same way God is patient with us.
Renee Jordan, Parents, Love Your Children

■

The child that never learns to obey his parents in the home will not obey God or man out of the home.   *Susanna Wesley*

■

Let parents bequeath to their children not riches, but the spirit of reverence.   *Plato*

■

We should strive to produce responsible adults who are able to function independently of parents' authority, yet wholly submitted to God's. If all goes well, they should become adults who live directly responsible to God within the limitations He has ordained.   *Charles Stanley,* How to Keep Your Kids on Your Team

■

The middle ground of love and control must be sought if we are to produce healthy, responsible children.   *James Dobson,* Dare to Discipline

■

Teach your child to hold his tongue. He'll learn fast enough to speak.   *Benjamin Franklin*

■

A wise son heeds his father's instruction.   *Proverbs 13:1*

■ ■ ■ ■ ■ ■ ■ ■ ■ ■ ■ ■ ■ ■ ■ ■ ■ ■

JUST LIKE YOU, DAD

Part of a father's role is to be a model of Christian
life in the world—a role loaded with
responsibility. Seek Christ's help to meet this challenge!

Be that yourself which you would bring others to be. Be it
with your whole being. . . . the power of example in a
parent does more to train a child than any other single
thing.   *Larry Christenson,* The Christian Family

■

There are little eyes upon you,
  and they're watching night and day,
There are little ears that quickly
  take in every word you say.
There are little hands all eager
  to do everything you do,
And a little child who's dreaming
  of the day he'll be like you. . . .
You are setting an example
  every day in all you do
For the little child who's waiting
  to grow up to be like you.
Unknown

■

Children have more need of models than of critics.   *Joseph Joubert*

45

■

Like father, like son. *Unknown*

■

Worship involves more than attending church or handing
out tracts. It means doing the best you can at whatever
you are doing, and being the best person you can be. We
are commanded to let our lights shine before men, and
there are many ways we can do that. Parents should make
sure their lights shine at home. *John Whitehead, in* How to
Raise Christian Kids in a Non-Christian World

■

A child's relationship to Jesus thrives in direct relation to
the obedience he gives to his parents. *Larry Christenson,*
The Christian Family

■

Children have never been very good at listening to their
elders, but they have never failed to imitate them. They
must; they have no other models. *James Baldwin*

■

Values are not *taught* to our children, they are *caught* by
them. *Unknown*

■

Parents who want their children to know God must cul-
tivate their own relationship with God. . . . Happy the
child who happens in upon his parent from time to time to
see him on his knees, who sees mother and father rising

early, or going aside regularly, to keep times with the
Lord.   *Larry Christenson,* The Christian Family

■

Example is a lesson that all can read.   *Gilbert West,* Education

■

Children are natural mimics—they act like their parents in
spite of every attempt to teach them good manners.
Unknown

■

Our children observe us all day long, at our best and at
our worst. They try to follow in our footsteps, copying
and mimicking us from the very beginning of their tender
lives. Much of what they learn comes simply from living
with us and observing us.   *Shirley Suderman, in* Parents and
Children

■

Parents who expect their children to follow in their
footsteps should be careful about dragging their feet.
Reverend George Hall

■

We live consistent Christian lives, not merely to set a
good example for our children, but because we believe
this pleases our Lord. . . . An ounce of loving role
modeling is worth a pound of parental pressure.
V. Gilbert Beers, in How to Raise Christian Kids in a Non-
Christian World

•

Successful parenting means: One, becoming what you should be. And two, staying close enough to the children for it to rub off. *Anne Ortlund,* Disciplines of the Home

•

I must be fit for a child's glad greeting,
His are eyes that there is no cheating;
He must behold me in every test
Not at my worst, but my very best;
He must be proud when my life is done
To have men know that he is my son.
Erwin Hirsch

•

O God, Bless our children with the spirit of love. May we so walk before them in love that Thy Spirit may use our example and our likeness to form them to Thy holy likeness. *Andrew Murray,* How to Raise Your Children for Christ

•

You can learn a lot just by watching. *Yogi Berra*

•

The example we parents set is probably our single most important act of guiding our families in this misguided world. . . . Discipling our children means more than leading moral lives. It means spending time with them so they see how we live out the gospel. . . . The goal in discipling our kids is to shape not only the way they think and believe but also the way they live. *Anthony T. Evans,* Guiding Your Family in a Misguided World

■

His heritage to his children wasn't words or possessions, but an unspoken treasure, the treasure of his example as a man and a father. *Will Rogers, Jr.*

■

The best way to teach character is to have it around the house. *Unknown*

■

Kids watch us closely. Every instant we spend with them helps them learn what motivates us. . . . we can talk about faith, but what we live shows the true faith behind the words. *Jay Kesler,* Energizing Your Teenager's Faith

■

Don't worry that your children never listen to you; worry that they are always watching you. *Robert Fulghum*

■

A child identifies his parents with God, whether the adults want that role or not. Most children "see" God the way they perceive their earthly fathers. *James Dobson,* The Strong-Willed Child

■

If we as parents are too busy to listen to our children, how then can they understand a God who hears? *V. Gilbert Beers, in* How to Raise Christian Kids in a Non-Christian World

■

There is never much trouble in any family where the children hope someday to resemble their parents. *William Lyon Phelps*, The Mother's Anthology

■

There is something in parenting that is more than principles. You may buy every book about parenting, catalog every principle, memorize the list, and even do your best to put these principles into your child's life. But there is something lost in translation unless principles become flesh and blood, heart and mind, and live themselves out in your life. *V. Gilbert Beers, in* How to Raise Christian Kids in a Non-Christian World

■

Any child will learn to worship God who lives his daily life with adults who worship Him. *Anna B. Mow*, Preparing Your Child to Love God

■

My parents showed me a lot about a gracious God. As a result, viewing God as a loving Parent hasn't been a difficult task. To me he is a God who, like my parents, not only has great expectations but who understands my limitations and readily gives needed encouragement. *Jean Sheldon*

■

One of the greatest desires children have is to grow up to be like Mom and Dad. Each new skill they learn, each new place they experience, each new phrase or word they define is a building block to maturity, and children instinctively know it. *Joyce Heinrich,* Making Summer Count

■

I can still look to the example my father set and get the sustenance I need. *Tyne Daly*

■

The hardest job kids face today is learning good manners without seeing any. *Fred Astaire*

■

Love is taught daily by example and by observation, in many little and big ways, in the things that we do for each other, and the things that we let others do for themselves. *Caryl Waller Krueger,* Six Weeks to Better Parenting

■

The imprint of the parent remains forever on the life of the child. *C.B. Eavey,* 2500 Sentence Sermons

■ ■ ■ ■ ■ ■ ■ ■ ■ ■ ■ ■ ■ ■ ■

HOME-BUILDER

The hours you spend in your home are all-important, both
for your family and for youself. The things you
do and the words you speak will either tear down
your house or build it up. Take care to be a home-builder.

Unless the LORD builds the house, its builders labor in
vain. *Psalm 127:1*

■

The domestic man, who loves no music so well as his
kitchen clock, and the airs which the logs sing to him as
they burn on the hearth, has solaces which others never
dream of. *Ralph Waldo Emerson*

■

When a man has children, the first thing he has to learn is
that he is not the boss of the house. I am certainly not the
boss of my house. However, I have seen the boss's job,
and I don't want it. *Bill Cosby,* Fatherhood

■

Charity begins, but does not end, at home. *Unknown*

■

Money can build or buy a house. Add love to that and you
have a home. Add God to that and you have a temple. You
have "a little colony of the Kingdom of Heaven." *Anne
Ortlund,* Disciplines of the Home

■

Once you own a home, you never run out of things to do on the weekends. *Unknown*

■

Home is a place where you can kick off your shoes. ✓
Charles Schultz, Home Is on Top of a Doghouse

'Mid pleasures and palaces
  though we may roam,
Be it ever so humble, there's
  no place like home.
J. Howard Payne

■

Home: A world of strife shut out, a world of love shut in.
Bob White

■

Character is like the foundation to a house . . . it is below
the surface.   *Unknown*

■

May you have warmth in your igloo, oil in your lamp, and
peace in your heart.   *An Eskimo benediction*

■

Whatever else may be said about the home, it is the bot-
tom line of life, the anvil upon which attitudes and convic-
tions are hammered out. It is the place where life's bills
come due, the single most influential force in our earthly
existence. . . . It is at home, among family members, that
we come to terms with circumstances. It is here life
makes up its mind.   *Charles R. Swindoll,* Home: Where Life
Makes Up Its Mind

■

Home is not a way station; it is a profession of faith in
life.   *Sol Chaniles,* The New Civility

54

A man's home is his hassle. *Paul D. Arnold* ✓

A man's home is his castle. It looks like a home, but it ✓
costs like a castle. *Milton Berle*

Definition of a home owner: a person who is always on
his way to the hardware store. *Unknown*

A palace without affection is a poor hovel, and the
meanest hut with love in it is a palace for the soul. *Robert
G. Ingersoll*

If I ever become a rich man,
Or if I ever grow old,
I will build a house with deep thatch
To shelter me from the cold.
Hilaire Belloc

The house of the righteous stands firm. *Proverbs 12:7*

The beauty of the house is order:
The blessing of the house is contentment:
The glory of the house is hospitality:
The crown of the house is godliness.
Fireplace motto

Good, honest, hard-headed character is a function of the home. If the proper seed is sown there and properly nourished for a few years, it will not be easy for that plant to be uprooted.   *George Dorsey*

Home, sweet home—where each lives for the other, and all live for God.   *T.J. Bach*

Home is where the heart is.   *Unknown*

Oh, that our home on earth might be to them the pathway, the gate to the Father's home in heaven! Blessed Father, let us and our children be Thine wholly and forever. Amen.   *Andrew Murray,* How to Raise Your Children for Christ

Parents have a job that requires lots of experience to perform and none at all to get.   *Unknown*

The strength of a nation, especially of a republican nation, is in the intelligent and well-ordered homes of the people. *Mrs. Sigourney*

Home to laughter, home to rest,
Home to those we love the best. . . .

Now the day is done and I
Turn to hear a welcoming cry.
Love is dancing at the door,
I am safe at home once more.
Unknown

∎

Home is where they send your bills.   *Charles Schultz,* Home ✓
Is on Top of a Doghouse

∎

No nation can be destroyed while it possesses a good
home life.   *J.G. Holland*

∎

If anyone serves, he should do it with the strength God
provides, so that in all things God may be praised through
Jesus Christ.   *1 Peter 4:11*

∎

He'd come home again to find it more
Desirable than it ever was before.   *Siegfried Sassoon*

∎

Home, nowadays, is a place where part of the family waits ✓
till the rest of the family brings the car back.   *Earl Wilson*

∎

We shall think of our home and family as His home, the
dwelling-place of His holiness.   *Andrew Murray,* How to Raise
Your Children for Christ

■

To be happy at home is the ultimate result of all ambition.
Unknown

■

Without hearts there is no home.   *Lord Byron*

■

There are only two lasting bequests we can hope to give
our children. One of these is roots; the other wings.
Hodding Carter

■

When there is room in the heart, there is room in the
house.   *Danish proverb*

■

Where we love is home.
Home, where our feet may leave but not our hearts.
Oliver Wendell Holmes

■

Home is where you don't have to make reservations in advance.   *Milton Berle*

■

Home is where you want to go after a hard day.   *Charles
Schultz*, Home Is on Top of a Doghouse

■

Babysitters are girls you hire to watch your television set.
Unknown

■

A home is a place where we find direction. *Gigi Graham* √
Tchividjian, Thank You, Lord, for My Home

■

The real art of living is beginning where you are. *Unknown*

■

The best time for parents to put the children to bed is
while they still have the strength. *Homer Phillips*

■

When the Spirit of God controls a person and, through
him, his family, that home, regardless of its circumstances, will experience the love, joy, and peace that everyone
yearns for and that God promises (Galatians 5:22-23). It is
not automatic, but comes as the result of a day-by-day
commitment to God and His principles. *Tim LaHaye,* The
Battle for the Family

■

To be happy at home is the ultimate result of all ambition;
the end to which every enterprise and labor tends and of
which every desire prompts the prosecution. *Johnson*

■

Nor need we power or splendor,
  Wide hall or lordly dome;
The good, the true, the tender,
  These form the wealth of home.
Mrs. Hale

A good laugh is sunshine in a house. *Thackeray*

■

Home is the place where the great are small and the small are great. *Robert C. Savage*, Pocket Quips

■

Home is the place there's no place like. *Charles Schultz*, Home Is on Top of a Doghouse

■

The best way to keep children home is to make the home atmosphere pleasant—and let the air out of the tires. *Dorothy Parker*

■

It may sound strange to speak of the relationship between parents and children in terms of hospitality. But it belongs to the center of the Christian message that children are not properties to own or rule over, but gifts to cherish and care for. Our children are our most important guests, who enter into our home, ask for careful attention, stay for awhile, and then leave to follow their own way. *Henri Nouwen*

■

I am sure that if people had to choose between living where the noise of children never stopped and where it was never heard, all the good-natured and sound people would prefer the incessant noice to the incessant silence. *George Bernard Shaw*, Misalliance

■

Your children need your presence more than your presents. *Jesse Jackson*

■

The wide world narrows to a road, ✓
   The wide road to a trail,
The trail a path to your abode,
   Some cabin in the vale;
The cabin narrows to a door.
   The little door is passed.
Then comes the heart you've hungered for—
   And you are home, at last.

Douglas Malloch

■

The most important thing a father can do for his children ✓
is to love their mother. *Kirk Douglas and Theodore Hesburgh*

■

A house is a machine for living in. *Charles Jeannert*

■

It is a wise father that knows his own child. *Unknown*

■

Happiness grows at our own firesides, and it is not to be
picked up in strangers' gardens. *Douglas Jerrold*

■

Providing for one's family as a good husband and father is ✓
a watertight excuse for making money hand over fist.

Greed may be a sin . . . but who can blame a man for "doing the best" for his children? *Eva Figes,* Nova

∎

There is no place more delightful than one's own fireside. *Cicero*

∎

I wanted a house that would have four bedrooms for the boys, all of them located some distance from the living room—say in the next county somewhere. *Jean Kerr,* Please Don't Eat the Daisies

∎

√ Home is the place where, when you have to go there, they have to take you in. *Robert Frost*

∎

And meadow rivulets overflow,
And drops on gate-bars hang in a row,
And rooks in families homeward go,
And so do I.
Thomas Hardy, "Weathers"

∎

√ Just about the time you think you can make both ends meet, somebody moves the ends. *Pansy Penner*

∎

It now costs more to amuse a child than it once did to educate his father. *Unknown*

■

If you make children happy now, you will make them happy twenty years hence by the memory of it. *Kate Douglas Wiggin*

■ ■ ■ ■ ■ ■ ■ ■ ■ ■ ■ ■ ■ ■ ■

ALL IN A FAMILY

Families give individuals a place to belong, a place to find
out their worth and identity, and a place to live out
the commands of God's Word. Thank goodness for the family!

It takes time to be a good father. It takes effort—trying,
failing, and trying again. *Tim Hansel,* What Kids Need Most in
a Dad

Learning to live with your family begins with a realistic
view of its possibilities and its problems. *Eugene Kennedy*

A family is a unit composed not only of children but of
man, woman, an occasional animal, and the common
cold. *Ogden Nash*

When you have children, it is not enough to put a roof
over their heads, food in their bellies, braces on their
teeth, stereo headphones on their ears, $35 jeans on their
bodies, and combs in their back pockets. You also have to
DO things with them. *D.L. Stewart,* Fathers Are People, Too

In order to pull together under one roof, all of us need
plenty of God's grace. *Ray and Anne Ortlund, in* Parents and
Children

·

Families come in different sizes and ages and varieties and colors. What families have in common the world around is that they are the place where people learn who they are and how to be that way. *Jean Illsley Clarke,* Self-Esteem: A Family Affair

·

Family is comfort in grief and joy in time spent together. *Unknown*

·

We grow our first and deepest roots within family and home; strong positive feelings about ourselves and firm emotional ties to others will anchor us in life, nourish our security, and permit us to weather successfully the adversities of our existence. *Bruno Bettelheim,* A Good Enough Parent

·

All happy families resemble one another; every unhappy family is unhappy in its own way. *Leo Tolstoy*

·

For no apparent reason, other than its functional value, the refrigerator became the meeting place of the American suburban family. It also became a frozen message center where anyone could drop by anytime of the day or night. The rules of communications via refrigerator were simple: Don't write with food in your hand. If phone numbers were illegible, be a sport. Messages left unclaimed over seven years would be destroyed.   *Erma Bombeck,* The Grass Is Always Greener Over the Septic Tank

■

√ Love is the first and most crucial ingredient for a balanced, harmonious family life. If love is freely given and freely accepted with no strings attached, individual freedom and responsibility can develop.   *Kay Kuzma,* Prime-Time Parenting

■

In your standard issue family . . . there are parents and there are children. The way you know which are which, aside from certain size and age differences and despite any behavior similarities, is that the parents are the bossy ones.   *Delia Ephron,* Funny Sauce

■

√ The family is God's idea, part of his loving plan for human well-being and joy.   *Maxine Hancock,* Creative, Confident Children

■

√ There are no perfect families.   *Kevin Leman*

■

If you aim to have a perfect family, you will be sorely disappointed. But you can create a strong family where the members respect each other, are loyal to one another, and enjoy being together.   *Judson Swihart, in* Parents and Children

∎

If there is one child and one toy, the child plays with the toy and makes no fuss about it. If there are two children and one toy there is a fight which has to be arbitrated by everybody in the house, including the cook, the yardman, and the woman who comes in on Tuesdays to iron. *Harold H. Martin,* Father's Day Comes Once a Year—and Then It Rains

∎

When the parents are becoming what God wants them to be, and the parents and children are spending a lot of time in their house together being a family, then the house becomes a home, and the home becomes an incubator for ideals, virtues, and visions. *Anne Ortlund,* Disciplines of the Home

∎

Educational television should be absolutely forbidden. It can only lead to unreasonable expectations and eventual disappointment when your child discovers that the letters of the alphabet do not leap up out of books and dance

around the room with royal-blue chickens. *Fran Lebowitz,*
Social Studies

■

Unity and diversity. Form and freedom. Togetherness
and individuality. A family. *Edith Schaeffer,* What Is a
Family?

■

Whatever is great and good in the institutions and usages
of mankind is an application of sentiments that have
drawn their first nourishment from the soil of the family.
Felix Adler

■

Someone has said, "Link a boy to the right man and he seldom goes wrong." I believe that is true. If a dad and his
son can develop hobbies together or other common inter-
ests, the rebellious years can be passed in relative tran-
quility. *James Dobson,* Parenting Isn't for Cowards

■

Insanity is hereditary. You get it from your kids.
Unknown

■

Nobody's family can hang out the sign, "Nothing the matter here." *Chinese proverb*

■

Laughter is the shortest distance between two people.
Victor Borge

■

One of the most tragic mistakes men make is to assume
that parenting is Mom's job. . . . Don't sit on the sidelines
or just show up for family events. Join the game. . . . Give
your children what they desperately need—yourself. *Bill
Peel and Mark Mahaffey*

■

Responsibility must be at the heart of loving within the
family. *Joseph and Lois Bird,* To Live as Family

■

Your family is unique. When God hand-picked your one-
of-a-kind spouse and your one-of-a-kind children, he gave
you the bond of family. *Joyce Heinrich and Annette LaPlaca,*
Making Summer Count

■

People who say they sleep like a baby usually don't have
one. *Leo Burke*

■

The definition of perfect parenting
  is easy to express,
Just err and err and err again
  but less and less and less.
Kay Kuzma, A Hug and a Kiss and a Kick in the Pants

■

Some people think that the amateurishness of family life
is the most widely distributed human beauty. *Harold
Brodkey, "A Largely Oral History of My Mother"*

■

Dad had dedicated his life to flipping off lights in rooms
with no one in them, turning off water spigots in the
bathroom, and throwing his body over the meter in an effort to stop the dials from spinning. His sermons on
saving money and energy fell on deaf ears. . . . His gospel
of utilities never got the respect he had hoped for. *Erma
Bombeck,* Family: The Ties That Bind . . . and Gag!

■

Parenthood is a process by which a pediatrician gets the
money that restaurants used to get. *Jacob M. Braude*

■

May mine be a family faith, exercising its influence on
my home, gaining and training all to walk with me. . . .
May mine be a truly consecrated home. *Andrew Murray,*
How to Raise Your Children for Christ

■

Fathering may be good for men as well as for children.
Ross D. Parke

■

As you pray together for needs inside and outside your im-
mediate family, concern for other family members in-
creases, joys and sorrows are commonly shared, and faith
is built as God sends the answers to prayer. *Joyce Heinrich
and Annette LaPlaca,* Making Summer Count

The family. We were a strange little band of characters trudging through life sharing diseases and toothpaste, coveting one another's desserts, hiding shampoo, borrowing money, locking each other out of our rooms, inflicting pain and kissing to heal it in the same instant, loving, laughing, defending, and trying to figure out the common thread that bound us all together. *Erma Bombeck,* Family: The Ties That Bind . . . and Gag!

How badly America needs husbands and fathers who are committed to their families—men who are *determined* to succeed in this important responsibility. *James Dobson,* Straight Talk to Men and Their Wives

The family begins in a commitment of love. *Joseph and Lois Bird,* To Live as Family

Your wife will be like a fruitful vine within your house; your sons will be like olive shoots around your table. Thus is the man blessed who fears the LORD.
Psalm 128:3-4

A happy family is but an earlier heaven. *Sir John Browning*

71

■

A strong family is one in which each member maintains a feeling of emotional togetherness with fellow members.... It is, in each member, an awareness of, and appreciation for, the family's uniqueness. *Barry and Patricia Bricklin, Strong Family, Strong Child*

■

Having a family is like having a bowling alley installed in your brain. *Martin Mull*

■

I have seen kids ride bicycles, run, play ball, set up a camp, swing, fight a war, swim and race for eight hours . . . yet have to be driven to the garbage can. *Erma Bombeck,* If Life Is a Bowl of Cherries, What Am I Doing in the Pits?

■

A man cannot leave a better legacy to the world than a well-educated family. *Thomas Scott*

■

Our most basic instinct is not for survival but for family. Most of us would give our own life for the survival of a family member, yet we lead our daily life too often as if we take our family for granted. *Paul Pearshall,* The Power of the Family

■

The quickest way for a parent to get a child's attention is to sit down and look comfortable. *Lane Olinghouse*

■

The family is a school for relationships. Along with providing food, shelter, and clothing, the family teaches its members how to get along with each other. . . . Growing up in a family, the most important lesson you learn is how to build ties with other people. *Mary Durkin,* Making Your Family Work

■

There is no failure that can alter the course of human events more than failing a family. *Eleanor McGovern*

The best place for a child to learn religious faith is at home, in the bosom of a family where faith is lived and practiced. *Dick Van Dyke, "Faith, Hope and Hilarity," in* Ideals

■

A happy childhood is one of the best gifts that parents have it in their power to bestow. *Mary Cholmondeley*

■

Who of us is mature enough for offspring before the offspring themselves arrive? The value of family is not that adults produce children but that children produce adults. *Peter DeVries*

■

No one can shoulder the responsibilities involved in being a full-time worker, parent, cook, and maid. And when a woman tries, either because she has to or because she wants to, everyone suffers. *Dr. Ronald Levant and John Kelly,* Between Father and Child

■

Large family, quick help. *Serbian proverb*

■

Your family—whatever the combination of humans under your roof—is a mystery, a marvel, a wonder. God has put you together, and things are happening in you and between you from day to day, from moment to moment. . . . God is powerfully at work. *Anne Ortlund,* Disciplines of the Home

■

Always laugh when you can; it is a cheap medicine. Merriment is a philosophy not well understood. It is the sunny side of existence.   *George Gordon Byron*

■

If I am committed to making my family strong and happy, then I won't collapse when pressures come along. Instead, I'll stick in there and work at building a healthy family.
Gary R. Collins, in Parents and Children

■

To the family—that dear octopus from whose tentacles we never quite escape, nor, in our inmost hearts, ever quite wish to.   *Dodie Smith*

■

Finally, all of you, live in harmony with one another; be sympathetic, love as brothers, be compassionate and humble.   *1 Peter 3:8*

■ ■ ■ ■ ■ ■ ■ ■ ■ ■ ■ ■ ■ ■ ■ ■ ■ ■

A MAN OF GOD

Between the demands of work and family life, it's hard
for a father to take time to consider who he is
before the Lord. Take some time out for yourself
and time out for God; renew your parenting and personal goals.

That best portion of a good man's life—his little, name-
less, unremembered acts of kindness and of love. *William
Wordsworth*

■

The greatest man is he who chooses the right with invin-
cible resolution; who resists the sorest temptations from
within and without; who is calmest in storms; and whose
reliance on truth, on virtue, on God, is the most unfalter-
ing. *Channing*

■

The righteous man walks in his integrity;
His children are blessed after him.
Proverbs 20:7, NKJV

■

He had lived by an uncompromising standard of devotion
to Jesus Christ. He had fought a good fight and kept the
faith until the end. *James Dobson about his father,* Straight Talk
to Men and Their Wives

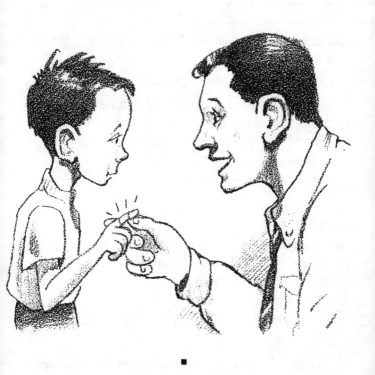

■

A gentleman is a gentle man. *Unknown*

■

A man can do only what he can do. But if he does that each day he can sleep at night and do it again the next day. *Albert Schweitzer*

■

God did not give us a spirit of timidity, but a spirit of power, of love, and of self-discipline. *2 Timothy 1:7*

■

Thrice noble is the man who of himself is king. *Phineas Fletcher*

■

Give us, O give us, the man who sings at his work! Be his occupation what it may, he is equal to any of those who follow the same pursuit in silent sullenness. He will do more in the same time—he will do it better—he will persevere longer. *Thomas Carlyle*

■

Blessed is the man
To whom his work is a pleasure,
By whom his friends are all encouraged,
With whom all are comfortable,
In whom a clear conscience abides,
And through whom his children see God. *Unknown*

■

The strength and happiness of a man consists in finding out the way in which God is going, and going in that way too. *Henry Ward Beecher*

■

Be strong and courageous. *Joshua 1:18*

■

I can never hide myself from me;
I see what others may never see;
I know what others may never know,
I never can fool myself, and so,

Whatever happens, I want to be
Self-respecting and conscience free.   *Edgar Guest*

■

When God measures a man, He puts the tape around the ✓
heart instead of the head.   *Unknown*

■

To be patient in little things, to be tolerant in large affairs,
to be happy in the midst of petty cares and monotonies,
that is wisdom.   *Joseph Fort Newton*

■

His divine power has given us everything we need for life
and godliness through our knowledge of him who called us
by his own glory and goodness. Through these he has given
us his very great and precious promises.   *2 Peter 1:3-4*

■

Pray every day for your children. This is an area where ✓
Christian parents don't have an option.   *Dick Hagstrom, in*
Parents and Children

■

Parentage is a very important profession; but no test of fitness for it is ever imposed in the interest of the children.
George Bernard Shaw

■

Acknowledge the God of your father, and serve him with
wholehearted devotion and with a willing mind, for the
LORD searches every heart and understands every motive

behind the thoughts. If you seek him, he will be found by you; but if you forsake him, he will reject you forever.
1 Chronicles 28:9

■

Whatever you do, work at it with all your heart, as working for the Lord, not for men, since you know that you will receive an inheritance from the Lord as a reward. It is the Lord Christ you are serving. *Colossians 3:23-24*

■

As long as I remind myself to appreciate breakfast with the children, driving through the park on the way to work, a pleasant evening meal, or a Saturday afternoon spent working in the garden, then happiness isn't around the corner, it's right in front of me. *Burton Hillis, "The Man Next Door," in* Better Homes & Gardens

■

Lead a quiet life . . . mind your own business . . . work with your hands . . . so that your daily life may win the respect of outsiders and so that you will not be dependent on anybody. *1 Thessalonians 4:11-12*

■

Do not pray for easy lives. Pray to be stronger men! Do not pray for tasks equal to your powers. Pray for powers equal to your tasks. *Keith L. Brooks,* The Cream Book: Sentence Sermons

■

Gladness of heart is the life of man, and the joyfulness of
a man prolongeth his days.   *Unknown*

■

[My children] make me totally dependent upon God. I can
do my best, but the ultimate results are out of my control.
My children help me run to God, the only safe place to be.
David Grant, "A Grace Assignment," in Christian Parenting Today

Every calling is great when greatly pursued. *Unknown*

The people I know who truly like themselves as persons, apart from their roles in life as husband, wife, parent, or job-holder, are those who have learned to be honest with themselves and who to some degree understand themselves. . . . Honesty with oneself, with God, and with one's fellow man is the first all-important step in spiritual and emotional growth. *Cecil G. Osborne,* The Art of Learning to Love Yourself

Be on your guard; stand firm in the faith; be men of courage; be strong. Do everything in love. *1 Corinthians 16:13-14*

Cheerfulness means a contented spirit; a pure heart, a kind and loving disposition; it means humility and charity, a generous appreciation of others, and a modest opinion of self. *Thackeray*

INDEX

87